YOU ARE ENOUGH
love poems
for the end of the world

RAF + ARAN,
I LOVE YOU.
Hu suk. + Qu·KN·

Smokii Sumac

for the warriors

to all my families,
to the ones who raised me, momma-bear, daddio, jenna, fil, kye and kayli, i miss
you all, every day,
to the ones who birthed me, anna, mel, mac, michele, steph, sam, kat, and patti,
to my sister, alex, and
to all my little cousins, i'm proud to come from our family.
to the ones who took me in,
shaawano, bryce, christy, baby, lacey, daphne, lily, brett, sage, mika, cleo, della,
& ike, i'm with you.
to our sun dance crew, clayton, annie, karina, amaya, aran, raf, and so many
more, you saved my life.
to roycie, winterhawk, and oh-hah-moe: hisses & kisses, and to abe, who takes
the best care, always,
thank you. i love you.

to my students,
the firekeepers, language speakers, future-teachers, poets, musicians, artists,
and, of course, the Kid. you're all going to change the world. you already are.
thank you.

to my teachers,
david sharp, bruce childs, kate reston, shelley little, and to jami macarty
especially, for starting me on the practice of daily haiku,
thank you.

to my therapists, become friends,
maria mckay and teresa howell, where would i be?
thank you.

to my besties,
keara, cryo, andrea, janelle(e-ell-e-ellioooo), shawnee (and will), mike b, sarah
(and spenny), meggan, christina, shawn(a), ceilidh, jon and vic, katie (and
freyja!), gwynnie, shawnee mcirogan, cori reed, ashley (and lu!), to scarlett,
heath, and especially kaz, for your work compiling, to ravon and junie b and
aster, to frankie, to jon and ej (and lucy), for believing in me, to cfsw 2017, the
first audience, to charlie, the first poem (pg 8) and to all the folks who make
nogojiwanong so special (you know who you are),
thank you.

to all my indigenous writer kin,
to kateri, and the team at kegedonce for this opportunity, and all your hard
work for 25 years! to leanne, daniel, warren, marrie, theo, rain, richard, cherie,
gregory, and so many more, for keeping the fire, to gwen, tenille, billy-ray,
lindsay, joshua, tanner, and jordan, for lighting it up,
and to all of you just coming up, or yet to write your first poems, i can't wait to
read your work.
thank you.

to the academics who might study and teach these words, (to terriann, who already has),
to my nals and ilsa families; miriam, scott, steve, brian, gambrasia, the davids (and carl), martha, karen, jessie, tria, gwen, james, twenter, nancy, deanna, sam, sophie, sarah, adar, june, and so very many more,
thank you.

to my mothers and grandmothers and aunties,
to all our mothers and grandmothers and aunties,
to tara and christa and leigh,
to catherine (and adam) and barb (and the old man) and meghan (and david),
to shari (and baby beaver)
to all the ones that created us,
thank you.

November 2018

Published by Kegedonce Press
11 Park Road
Neyaashiinigmiing, ON N0H 2T0
www.kegedonce.com
Administration Office / Book Orders
P.O. Box 517
Owen Sound, ON N4K 5R1

Printed in Canada by Ball Media
Cover photo collage, back cover
author's photo and section page photos:
Smokii Sumac
Sun dance crown illustration:
Cleo Keahna
Design: Chantal Lalonde Design

Library and Archives Canada Cataloguing in Publication

Sumac, Smokii, 1988-
[Poems. Selections]
    You are enough : love poems for the end of the world / Smokii Sumac.

ISBN 978-1-928120-16-2 (softcover)

    I. Title.

PS8637.U569A6 2018   C811'.6   C2018-905741-6

For Customer Service/Orders
Tel 1-800-591-6250 Fax 1-800-591-6251
100 Armstrong Ave. Georgetown, ON L7G 5S4
Email orders@litdistco.ca

We acknowledge the support of the Canada Council for the Arts, which last year
invested $153 million to bring the arts to Canadians throughout the country.

Canada Council   Conseil des arts
for the Arts   du Canada

We would like to acknowledge funding support from the Ontario Arts
Council, an agency of the Government of Ontario.

ONTARIO ARTS COUNCIL
CONSEIL DES ARTS DE L'ONTARIO
an Ontario government agency
un organisme du gouvernement de l'Ontario

Previously published:
this is what they felt, page 42, *The Capilano Review 3.30.*
there are hierarchies of grief, pp. 46-47, *Canadian Literature,* pp. 230-231.
how to support me today, pp. 56-57, *Electric City Magazine,* June 27, 2016.
after dm, p. 101, Dylan Miner's limited edition book,
aanikoobijigan//waawaashkeshi, 2017.

All previous publications were published under Smokii Sumac's former name,
Angela Semple.

table of contents

#nogoseries

poems from and for you,
nogojiwanong

i.

nogo has become
a place where
when i walk home
many friends appear

reminiscent of
my hometown
in its close fam-
iliarity

you
new as i was once
join me in walking
and stopping
to say many hellos

"famous" you noted
as we met her there
she laughed
then (knowing)
smiled

peterborough famous
GE shutting down
in the
electric city

ii.

two years in nogo
brought me friends with a cottage
learning river life

crickets and frog songs
the way the water reflects
black blue silver moon

iii.

such a perfect day
i'm glad i spent it with you
it's a lou reed haiku

this weekend's highlights:
covering come my way by
tara williamson

when kwe came on stage
and we sang in harmony
with a new guitar

learning to breathe
trusting you pushing open
the weight in my chest

leaving my handprint
that something to hold on to
reading poetry

seeing all of you
i haven't seen for so long
conway behind the bar

you and i laughing
at our matching red plaids in
the garnet's familiar light

iv.

sarah mcneilly
and spencer allen singing
in their living room

make me believe in
magic and love i just had
to write a haiku

v.

for victoria mohr-blakeney

locked in a way
bodies tired carry us
move us house us safe
love watching you dance
remembering miracles
how we grow stretch lift
together stronger
we meet after your show
you share your honest practice
i share love stories
we drink hot tea
hang ornaments on the tree
not our memories
yet we make new ones
then

now
a year later and
we reminisce on how we
connected that night
your first christmas since
your mother died
me now grieving my own
we talk funeral homes
and unwitting strangers
in airport bathrooms and
grocery store lineups
sorry about what happened

vi.

qałsa
(or)
three years
the other day a friend said
"it's funny how integrated you are"
i laughed and said
"assimilated."
but the truth is i was born here
and my spirit must have remembered
the way the leaves set the trees
on fire in manomin season
the humid air
familiar to my newborn lungs
the big water
first to welcome me here
must have been calling me back
i must have known somewhere
in my subconscious as i drove out east
that the lakes would teach me
what the mountains could not
the same way the aunties will share
what my mothers did not

there's a new moon now
i used to write you poems
when the full moon came
tonight i'm writing
for the night swimming
for the good coffee
for recognition
their spirits seeing my own
for odenabe
for the medicine
passed back and forth and through us
healing us with gifts
tonight i'm writing
for the necklace you wear and
your sister's fat cat
writing for you
too
and our little brightest star
honouring your birth
writing this for them
the newest string of this web
curating relations
migwech to nogo
this place we come to gather
this place brought me you
and somehow i see
it's also bringing me
me

viii.

it's been three whole years
since i set out on the road
everything in the car
crossing the country
visiting on the way
figuring it out
three years i've been here
this place
nogojiwanong
three apartments, too
i got to know you
went to your shows and said hi
now i sing along
it takes this much time
to know the roads leading home
to know where to eat
know where to cross streets
to avoid unwanted crowds
know who you can call
to fall in and out of love
acquire exes
and some best friends, too
to help with the break ups
takes this kinda time
to make yourself
home

three years to make home
and here i am wondering
where the next place will
be

#courting

on dating and gender and
falling in (and out) of love

somedays it's the (big)
little things; the best first date
an added bus route

                                            you
                                       inanimate
                                             me
                                       it's okay
                                      i move fast
                               returning summer

late august ripened
tomato she picked when i
saw her this morning

"a gift" but you have
to eat it with salt perfect
summer closing night

we went up to the
roof of the parkade slept in
a tent in the rain

                                  i'll invite you in
                      come kiss my changing colours
                            sun on autumn leaves

i saw my best friend
in transit and then later
i liked kissing you

                             sometimes all you need
                             a beautiful flirtation
                               teeth on bottom lip
                             dreaming of thailand
                     of brown eyes and the middle
                               a hug and a smile
                            and knowing that you
                       will be watching the sunrise
                              while i am asleep

hair swept just over
your eye
dusky midnight dark
waning in the clouds

                                        i tried to write you
                                  an "i like you" haiku but
                            these nerves they take my voice

just cold enough for
a jacket i changed outfits
three times so nervous
i thought about it
a million times
better
than i imagined
and now the replays
over and over writing
shit poems here and
keeping the good ones
for myself

                                        it's snowing again
                                light cold kisses and talks
                                          of relationships
                            with the earth with sky with
                                    one another with
                                    consent and active
                                          decolonial
                      intent//action like snowflakes
                                    kissing down on us
                                    your hair my lips
                            inviting each other in
                                    eating together
                                    creating family

for the love of all
that is queer and brown for those
beautiful disabled bodies
for those wedding rings
flashing on husbands fingers
men so deeply in
love with each other
a femme with glasses and bangs
held onto my glance
later i wept through
readings of learning to love
ourselves our bodies
each of our naked
burning hearts our lipstick and
our binders our canes
our love
this one is simply
for all of our love which can
never be wrong

for kl

inclusivity
in its purest form i think
denies all labels
yet some labels
we wear proud pins on lapels
impossible not
to categorize
for communicative ease
break the barrier

there's no gender here
equal parts truth in balance
no need for power

and it's just like that
wednesday becomes favourite
afternoons with you

i am a they / them
i say then promptly erase
the assertion (she
her accepted too)
in case it makes you falter
you uncomfortable
i backstep so quick
you'd think I danced salsa
it's harder in public
i'll be woman if
it's easier on you if
you think it's sexy
fishnets and low cuts
because the three-piece suit is
also energy
and i'm just so tired
you probably think this song is
about you but i
want you to know it's
really about me queer bright
ktunaxa and proud
two spirit is a
responsibility a
relationship with
all of creation
but most of all with myself
and i'm just learning
to be kind to be
unapologetic so
please let me breathe deep
into who i am
please don't take it personal
it's not you it's me
me who i like more
now without the trying
too hard to please

you find parts of me
like the sun finds open space
deep in the mountains

pressure lung heavy
cold toes hard air frozen sharp
too thin you not there

can you see an end?
your eyes just lighter than mine
smile agreeing
no

believe we can be
february in the woods
june on the west coast

a wave of your hand
nightmares have lasted all night
let's dream while we can

stop in to kiss you
leave medicine to get you
through til i return

ʔa·s k̓ȼiɬmitiɬnukqa
two moons have passed us
waxing full waning new and
back here full again
two moons have passed us
since we first came together
shared a kiss said yes
two moons have passed us
though it's really the same moon
showing herself twice
in full bodied awe
when i witness her as when
i look at you love
two moons have passed us
she's unchanged it's us who grow
with each new reveal
learn to sing shout it
learn to sit quiet listen
sometimes neither well
other times we breathe
move the ocean together
keep each other warm

qaɬsa ȼiɬmitiɬ natanik̓
three moons have passed us
filled up with light and emptied
then poured full again
three moons of learning
wolf moon
snow moon
worm moon now
three moons of growing
celebrate with seeds
reading words to each other
your voice painting scenes
next chapter my turn
this book closest to my heart
this piece of beauty
reading like three moons
decoding the underlines
sometimes we just guess
giggle at desire
bodies more than distraction
languages of love
nicknames and our songs
more than a few trips away
three moons of being
coming together
not into one like the moon
instead like two calls
over the water
two wings skimming the surface
three moons
me with you
ka nuqɬukin

xa·ȼa ȼiɬmitiɬ nukqa
four moons have passed us
looked bright and full right at us
turned away again
tides rising falling
there's magic in reflection
in the ocean pull
whispers in the dark
your fingers run through my hair
skim over fretboards
weather gets warmer
passing spring equinox
leave windows open
learn to let air in
remember to breathe together
to talk it out
we stay up all night
stories shared like our first moon
feels so nice
like love
giggle cheeks blushing
at our inside jokes nicknames
you, ka nuqɬukin
there's nobody else
nobody i would rather
invite sit beside
at all those awkward
events i should have said no to
still we are learning
still you make me laugh
still i don't want to leave you
but i'll be back soon

sunday before sleep
thinking of your clear boiled down
sap sugar brown eyes
commune dreaming though
we'll find a word that fits more
something like nogo
something like ode
something like this place my heart
your smile "i like you"
somewhere crushes grow
where every day we love
and some days we cry
as i lay me down
in this spot i left last night
to come find you there
to come trust you there
thinking of our weekends filled
like buckets on trees
like dirty bathtubs
after we wash the dog like
courting with love poems

dirty leaves rake clean
fallen fizzing fermented
we do the yard work
you show me the shed
i hear your eyes light up dreams
you see future here
and i am in it
we plan my birthday party
i play with the dog
you fill pots with soil
seedlings soon to start waking
like your quiet heart
under the cold moon
we would keep each other warm
under the covers
now like the dark earth
we soften slowly open
laugh hard smile often
cheeks sore from happy
like when it's still chilly out
blushing red with spring

when you don't see me
i try not to care so much
i know who i am
i lived it today
on the radio
on stage
in the sugar bush
i lived it today
in the turnaround which you
maybe didn't see
maybe too busy
maybe i just kept it for myself
doing the hard work
like letting go by
trusting those who will answer
being trustworthy
sharing our stories
i have chosen family
and they?
they see me

                              there was a last time
                i drove through these same mountains
                              you and me it was

                              then

                              and now it's us
                              new family together

                              this will be last time
                              the next time we come

pull into their driveway
greeted with a sleepy hug
familiarity
they pour a glass of water
take care of me
a soft catching up
more to come soon
the cats make their sounds
humidity coating my skin
home again
home

and they told me now
you are head over heels
now
enamoured with her
another
not me
and i still hear your anger
feel criticism
under my thin skin
this cancer moon emotion
still whispers to me
your voice still in my head
while you
they say
enamoured
and i wonder now
if you even asked
yourself about me before
you fell in love now
did you justify?
use my silence to pretend
you didn't hurt me?
always all my fault
i wonder if you'll thank me
for finding her now
how long did you wait?
when you broke my boundaries
had you loved her yet?
was that why you tried
so damn hard to reach me now?
so you could tell me?
like you told them then
when I was still new and you
still enamoured

thought i was past it
then i caught a glimpse of you
my heart in my throat
going much too fast
like in the car yesterday
like it used to be
only now i know
how to tell myself to breathe
i know it will pass
even when i'm sure
it'll stop right in my chest
i can remember
i've survived it
so many times before this
only one time more
breathe in and out in
the bathroom stall and it will
pass
text my best friends
it will pass it will
probably never for good
it always comes back
but maybe next time
when i see you it won't hit
so god damned hard it
won't feel like this one
i won't have to talk me down
for as long
next time

two days ago now
someone posted your photo
almost perfect numb
"oh they still exist"
the thought floating in my mind
surprised at presence
since avoiding you
is a game i win
only
lost twice
since july
numbness not the goal
it's disassociation
not really healing
not really breathing
i sobbed in bed that day too
told myself it was
not because of you
of course
each memory now
a poem you're in
but as i read them
it strikes me
you were always
the periphery
on this day last year
one small example
i wrote
haiku about her
her who is still here
sure
there's mention of you there
but clear to me now
i knew what mattered
even then
when i was still convinced
what we had was love

at 29 i lie naked on the beach and think of you

as i undress the fear knots in my stomach like every time your words
threatened to cut the fleshy parts of me

blood rushing to the surface threatening to pour out of me

at 29 i climb up off my towel the whole brown body of me
and walk the length of the beach to the ocean

i laugh as i wonder if anyone's noticing the canucks tattoo on my ass
you never understood my love of hockey

always looked at me like a stranger when you found out i liked
something you couldn't understand

my cheeks redden as i notice an older man down the beach, his body
hardening as he watches me. breath rising within me my shoulders
straighten and i show him all of me. i can hear your voice now.

"gross."

you would have sneered, as i enjoyed this moment of validation. his
erection reminding me of this body i am in and the power it can hold.
he doesn't advance upon me, just sits, his erection and my knowing
between us.

i am someone you could never understand.

the water is cold
cold enough that when it hits my chest i'm gasping for breath

i was always gasping for breath at the coldness of you

the salt of my tears meets the salt of the ocean and for a moment i think
i'm going to cascade myself into the depths disappearing forever lost
amidst the waves of your sharp edges

and i am filled with rage

and migizi comes

and i am here

at 29 naked in the ocean and migizi and his brother are flying overhead
and i am presenting myself to them and i see the gasping is not like you
not like those choking suffocating moments where your eyes could shut
me up where your words sliced my skin like the razors did so well back
when i was the age you are stuck in now.

no.

this gasp is like the one i took bursting forth from the womb of a woman
who wouldn't even look at me

who somehow gave me a name and then passed me off to the foster
mother

remember that christmas dinner at the table when my sister
nonchalantly handed my adoption papers to my mom who opened
them, looked for a second, said "oh, these are yours" and passed them to
me?

"don't read them now, you'll probably cry."

and i am filled with rage.

and i saw you on instagram smiling at pride.

you, the baby dyke
that doesn't even like going down.

and i am filled with rage

and i am in this place

the cedars surround me

the ravens chatter

i am the sun on my skin and the brown of it all

the brown resting on

this ktunaxa skin

at 29

i'm naked on the beach
and thanking the eagles above me the water around me the sun on my
skin the sand and the trees
that

you're
not
here.

poets get crushes
maybe more than average?
we tend to fall hard
what is a poem?
i asked my class on monday
the room went silent
don't make eye contact
internet definition
talks about feelings
poets good at that
the emotion of the thing
"you just care too much"
"and that's a good thing"
i followed your lead today
sent a crush text, too
not to them
they know
we've established my desire
and boundaries too
respecting their bounds
leaves me seeking new crushes
a poets new muse
this month brought the past
"i was always into you"
"why didn't we date?"
before i was queer
no, before i knew i was
before i saw truth
but here we are now
inspired by young poets
to profess a crush
so i'll tell you, dear
i've got so many crushes
so very many
poems yet to write

haiku
consent series or
#makesexgreatthefirsttime

i.

forget the bad sex
i want to read the good
the genderless space
they made art with snakes
took a break from installing
to meet me
drink tea
them smiling sexy
"can i kiss you?" I asked them
"yes"
and then we are
in that moment first
when your insides cross fingers
the inhale
connect
lips on collar bone
the length of them along you
move from couch to stand
tiptoes
"you're so tall"
"do you want to go in here?"
"Yes."
move to the bedroom
slow for seconds
sneak kisses between giggles
feeling deep sweet shy
check in again now
hand sweeping near that soft spot
where pants meet stomach
inhale deep soft kiss
hard exhale you think of snakes
of hands on the wheel
on you
shed clothing
"i really like your arms" flex
feel stronger here now
fall into laughter
in this bed
neither of us
will sleep in for long

ii.

my first time was good.
when i say this to women
they are often shocked
we are taught instead
it should hurt
that it's breaking
something inside you
not taught our pleasure
only shame
turn the lights off
normal is for him
did you get him off?
wait through long pounding hours
or just-a-minutes (this never happens)
taught to hold our breath
stare at how many ceilings
to-do list in mind
my first time was good
the consensual first time
the one that i count
he smelled so damn good
had softest high thread count sheets
made crepes when we woke
(yeah
i stayed the night)
and isn't that what we need?
radical balance
i wish that for you
a revolution of sex
for every human
softest sheets and crepes
or rose petals and candles
tender exploring
whatever you like
maybe punk rock and the floor
if it turns you on
creating the world
each ask
each yes at a time
co-write the story

iii.

the other first time
her name whispers on my tongue
taste sweet green apples
she walked in the room
in my memory it's like
she was sent to me
a gift for my truth
that feels admitted right then
yep
i like women
when i say a gift
don't get me wrong here, okay?
a gift of learning
reciprocity
not consuming capital
a gift in our way
desire so sweet
when you don't seek to own her
only make her smile
we tangled ourselves
into the web we knew then
starbucks and late nights
dancing clean
sober
at the recovery club
driving in my car
turning it up loud
she had tattoos everywhere
and then she kissed me
that other first time
the Godfather our soundtrack
hard film our soft light
remember the way
she melted into you there
you were so damn scared
and yet each small ask
"is this alright?" met with yes
you kissed each tattoo
became lovers then
while the godfather played on
you learned about her
you
us together
that other first time
sweet green apple
consent

iv.

last night in the car
you checked in on my feelings
such care and concern

i thought about
toxicity in language
of that word "friendzone"

i know how men feel
guess what? i've too, been "rejected"
not just their problem

but in those moments
i've learned to take what is mine
hold my own feelings

honour yours
truly
when you tell me what you need
listen and hear you

we can't just seek yes
convincing ourselves worthy
only through your eyes

you

we decide
without really knowing
already

"the one"

last night in the car
you checked in on my feelings
and i was honest

you here in my life
brings this magic
this grounding

there's a new strength here
quiet flirtations
fields of blooming trees

you are incredible
you teach me to see
the world through your careful lens

glimpses of beauty
you point out to me
things i rush past too quickly

you slow me right down

last night in the car
when i checked my own feelings
i told you the truth

everything we share
all the beauty you can give
you as you are here

you
are enough

and you deserve above all
your autonomy

so if i ask you
like i did
if there's more here
and you say no

then my friend thank you
for what you give is enough

remove the pressure
im only here for
what you choose to give freely

grateful for friendzone
since it's where we're
both comfortable

where we
mutually find
consent

when you wake up there
all my ex west coast lovers
you'll see there was news
the ocean a threat
to your warm sleeping bodies
you awakening
to cancelled warnings
i'll text my best friend
say "whoah"
she's who i thought of
and then it was you
in your various places
where i remember
scattered near the drive
that studio work/live space
near the chicken
factory
your place around the corner
with the vinyl collection
your mothers house
your twin bed
above the garage in coquitlam
that apartment in new west
where you made me crepes
perhaps because i've
been writing poems after you
when i heard the news
i saw the waves crash
while you slept in my memories
of the places
i used to visit

"i was thinking about the stars and could not get you off"
poem after tea and jojo

a month on testosterone and you realize you can
hit that app

you are a trans tribe grindr dream
question\\ftm//question

"do you have a penis or a vagina?"
question
"i love bonus hole boys"
question

and then they slide into the dms and later they'll slide into you and you'll
breathe quietly

moan question
consent moan
question
consent

this is the first time since you changed your name that you've taken a lover

\\question
you're in the art gallery director's apartment in kingston a place you could
never find again unless your google search remembers.

there's a giant owl in the corner that reminds you of your aunt eva.

there's no gender here
you drink black tea and talk about the person who lives here
the man with the owl who is currently in iceland.

\\question

"am i your first grindr date?"

yes.
yes.
yes.
\\question.

"can i kiss you?"
and as you drive away
you press play and listen to st.vincent's new album in it's entirety.
masseduction\\ *i can't turn off*
what turns me on

the night before our first date i went to the sex store in the plaza and then drove around chasing the sunset so i could take a picture for you

the sex store in our town (it's a city, they always say) is called forbidden pleasures

of course as i pull up
i laugh
a week ago we were carving out hard lines
"we can't do this."
the ethics of the thing feeling creepy for me and recognized by you

power dynamics
google age gaps
did you know beyoncé and jayz have twelve years between them?

think of all the older men who took me
who i chose

some of them
still good stories

what kind of story do i want to be?

my ex kept my old harness in one last power play when i left them.
i decided it wasn't worth going back into the fire to retrieve. it was a
forest fire. the kind that threatened to suffocate me before i burned up.

a week ago we switched the boundary
we couldn't last
not talking

but we wouldn't see each other

okay
set
agreed upon

last night when i came out of the sex store with my little black bag hoping
i didn't run into anyone i knew i was taken by the light in the sky

there was a time when i prayed for presence

a time i begged the spirits to help me free myself so that i could witness
the beauty around me

i began following the streets
north
and west

north
and west

trying to find a piece of sky big enough to show you

it was on a darkening cul-de-sac full of big fancy houses (not really my
style even if I am kinda bougie) that i realized i had to find the highest
point.

my friend makes films about buffalo. she talks of how they always go to
the highest point. there's a story in this.

and so i chased the sunset driving against my instinct back east and
south and up that big hill past the teaching lodge where i went to my
first full moon ceremony to pray for the journey this body was about to
start
and i reached the spot
where amongst all the drinking teens in their big trucks and the couples
making out i took a picture and sent it to you

"so you can see what i see."

when i got home i put on my new harness and wore it around the house
the way autostraddle told me to when i was a baby queer (truly, not long
ago)

and this morning
i lie naked in my bed
thinking of sunsets
and sunrises
this one marking
the beginning of the day I'll see you
our first date

all the clocks blinking

and i laugh to myself now
remembering you
me
so enamoured
first sweet kisses hold me close
there's nothing but you

we didn't even
notice
the power was out
til it came back on

"do you want to take the Cadillac for a ride?"
Or: a love letter to Transthetics
the company that made my prosthetic dick

From the first time I saw your video I knew that this was *the One*.

Ordered it on the next weekly release date and felt butterflies driving to shoppers to pick up the package I had missed at my door when it came.

Chase Ross, youtuber and trans 101er said he cried when he used his for the first time.

A trans friend once said it best "being trans is expensive" as they waved their hand gesturing to their shelf of dicks.

I ordered two new binders that day, too. I mean why not? if you're gonna do it...

Right for me was binder and shirt on. I shudder as I think of cis dudes with a shirt and no pants on, but this is the body I'm working with and I currently feel sexiest with a binder on under a button down.

I've already prepped three pairs of fancy new underwear (also ordered online) the way you showed in the video, elastic sewed in to hold my new body part in place. As I fit the elastic around it I can feel the gentle rise of anxiety and... adrenaline? That sense of impending adventure like sitting in a cart waiting for a rollercoaster to start, or filling up at the gas station, your last stop on the way out of town.

self love is a revolution for an NDN
I say out loud and think of Quill Christie Peters.

"self love is a revolution for an NDN"
and I hear Tenille Campbell's laugh.

"Self Love is a Revolution for an NDN"
and i take a deep breath
and I look down

and I am transformed.

*

I didn't cry after.
but I did text my friend three days and countless orgasms later

"I'm having the best sex of my life. By myself."

Chase Ross said the first time he used his with a partner, he cried again.

at some point I start telling people
"I've got the Cadillac of dicks."

I shudder when I think of a cis dude professor I know drunkenly
repeating over and over to a room full of colleagues
I have a huge dick.

I consider what it means to write erotic poems about my dick.

I wonder if it's the same.

My best friend brings me to the reason I write: "but would you want to
hear another trans poet read that poem?"

> *Yes.*
> *I would.*

And then there's a moment of electricity between me and a woman.
She's on my couch. We've been friends for awhile, but I hadn't
considered

> *This.*

There's a need so deep in my body to lean over and lie my head in her
lap that I'm nearly shaking in the effort to stop it. I hold back. Other
people in the room. We begin texting incessantly later on. For eight days
we text incessantly.

And then we are meeting in the city. And then we are kissing. And then?

I'm explaining the nuances of queer sex and telling her about

> *the Cadillac.*

I shake my head and laugh because what man has this much confidence
about his dick in the hours before he's about to lose his virginity?

It was kind of like losing my virginity again.

Of course, never assuming it would happen I just kept kissing and asking and she kept kissing and saying yes and asking me and I kept saying yes until she smiled

You know that smile.

The one with the raised eyebrow that says there is nothing in this world I want more than to do this next thing I'm going to do to you

And with that eyebrow and her eyes that have flecks of gold in them like when the sun hits the water just right sparkling she leans in and asks

"can we take the Cadillac for a ride?"

and with her,
I am transformed.

#theworld

a constant state of grief

Grief. *(after billy-ray)*

after grief after
grief after grief after grief
after grief after

                                        it's all i can hear
                                  babies crying for mothers
                                         feel it in my chest
                                         in blood memory
                        as white parents laugh when their
                                  kid throws a tantrum
                                       take candy away
                        but hug and hold and comfort
                                  because they are there
                        while brown children scream
                        their parents locked in a cell
                                  god knows how far
                                                    away

"tender age shelters"
for babies and young children
no words
only tears

                                        do not be fooled by
                        their false claims of allyship
                                  we are still at war.

returning sadness
another pipeline project
another body

                                        and my heart is in
                                  standing rock as family
                                    gather to fight war
                                         protector is a
                        word you should learn it's not called
                                             protesting
                                               it's love

this is what they felt
our great grandparents as those
indian agents
stormed their houses and took
our grandparents\\their children
this is what they felt
our ancestors on
the same land we stand on now
at custer's violence
this is what they felt
watching the caribou drown
the waters dammed
the buffalo gone
hunger in our hearts for our
relations\\all of them
this is what i feel
grenades and rubber bullets
pepper spray and dogs
dogs are medicine
weapons once came from the land
turned them against us
this is what they felt
this is what i hope you feel
for we need you now

and i've seen the news
in saskatchewan but i
have no words for now

#JusticeforColten
it's time you recognize
Our humanity

what you don't understand
is that for the Indigenous person in your life
Colten is family.
Colten is me.
Colten is my brother.
Barbara
is my mom's name.
Barbara is my auntie.
Barbara is our grandma.
Tina is our niece
our little sister
our baby girl.
What you don't understand is
when you survive genocide
everyone left
is family.

super blue blood moon
they're calling it in whiteness
and i have to search
the internet to
seek anishinaabe names
spirit moon
i think now
because bear moon seems
too early but
what do i know
i know colten's name
the trial starting now
my heart in saskatchewan
my heart here
about to teach billy-ray
to walk into a classroom
and say colten's name
barbara's name
last week
john t. williams'
name
i dreamt of bleeding
all night
dreams of blood

preparing to fly
back across these so many
nations
and i know
there will be sobbing
i hope my seat mates are folks
with blood like my own
or just folks with friends
like me and my family
so that maybe if
i can't hold it in
they will understand
why
maybe they'll cry too
this country's problem
is pretty clear to me now
a problem of grief
we know to grieve it
you settler
it's clear do not
instead of asking us
"what can i do?"
or even "hey, how are you?"
instead of waiting
send a quick message
any words of comfort help
don't expect response
instead of fearing
always the wrong thing
just act out of love

flying here today
forces the remembrance
this prairie home
where i lived one time
medicating myself hard
from the deepened pain
being NDN
in saskatchewan
too much
for this mountain heart
i can taste the booze
now in the back of my throat
smell it in the air
how do you cope now?
find a spot to burn sweetgrass
and say Colten's name

there are hierarchies of grief

on days like these my heart thinks of you;

> when the rest of the world grieves for a world they think is gone,
> when we've awoken to a nightmare we didn't think was possible,
> when i am afraid that i can't make it to the next sunrise and i
> don't know if the tears will ever stop,
> when smiling seems like it might be a failure.

on days like these i find strength in your presence—

> like a lighthouse on fire in a storm i
> couldn't find my way out of alone.

You once told me the kitchen floor is the best place to cry;

recommended crawling to the refrigerator and crying to the beat of its
hum.
gave us all songs to introduce us to the grief you fell in love with,
your generosity flowing from fingertips on that piano you don't play, in
poems and recordings, wrapping it's arms around me, and telling all of us
we can stay.
it is possible even when you've known
a grief such as this.

you told me i was like your child, so close to his age;

opened the door and hugged me and let me lie hungover on your couch
until i got sober again.
texted "i need you" and trusted me enough to ask for help.
you were honest when you told me you needed to go to his gravesite
alone;
it's his mommy time.
you gave me the only picture i have of he and i together told me stories
of memories i don't have anymore, and you gave me three more cousins,
too.
to hug and to hold and to laugh with and even if i don't see you enough
you've given me family here.

and on days like these i think of you, my girl;
the length of you wrapped in scarves and borrowed jewelry, a skirt
made of stars.

> i think of the trust you refuse to stop giving as you get
> in the car on the bus on the plane i think of the ocean
> your voice keeping us warm like the mediterranean
> sun\ \back in september when i went to the west coast
> i found some little path to the ocean between great big
> houses on our way to the ferry so i could swim for you
> both.

i think of shooting stars
of our star
of the way you laugh
and how you get
quiet.

> i think of how you taught me to carry and take care of
> the feathers, and showed me where your little star so
> strong brought down a tree so we could be with the
> water.

on days like these, my girl,
i close my eyes and listen for your harmonies,
as we learn to sing together in north dakota,
in flint michigan, somewhere in wisconsin,
where you kept us warm and i kept us covered,
where you kept us fed and i kept us moving.

on days like these my heart thinks of you and the love i am filled with
because you are here.
and i know there have been mornings worse than this one.
i know that there is more strength in us than we can ever imagine.
i know that the only truth is the sun will rise and fall and rise again,
spring will come and winter and fall again, and i'll keep giving and
loving and singing and crying and swimming and visiting.
i'll keep on.

hu sukɬq̓ukni ʔaɬ ka manaɬa
thank you, our mothers,
i love you.

ał ka manała
our mothers
taken from us
look at these photos
read our stories now
weep with us
give us your tears
those tears medicine
get uncomfortable
choose one of her names today
write it on paper
carry it with you
know that she is the land here
she is the water
each moment you take
to admire the changes
the autumn leaves bring
remember her name
each breath you borrow from the trees
remember her name
you ask what to do
and i'm telling you now
learn to share sorrow
grieve with us
hold her
your guilt is useless to me
your tears
medicine

                              our trained bodies know
                          dangerous men the way they
                                won't listen let up
                                        distance
                                       keep calm
                                         but no
                            body will come so you de
                                 escalate and stall
                                until a safe berth
                       is reached wide enough and far
                                 with people around

after katherena vermette
"a past like hers" this
a thousand moments echo
"incidents" strange men
familiar men
be afraid even before
you have memories
"situations" these
flashbacks seeing blood on snow
handprint bruises dark
every cough season
a reminder she can't breathe
bruises on her chest
visible to her
the blood still under new snow
and yet she's lucky
one of the lucky
not missing not murdered
just "a past like hers"

                                 if i can't trust men
                       (and trust me i've tried to find
                            men who deserve trust)
                             without trusting men
                                how do i become
                                         a man
                                 worthy of trust?

nothing but awake
clear familiar aching
body's spring cleaning
been waiting to bleed
feel the deep need of release
middle of the night
draw a hot bath
send painvoice up into sky
dark heat woman song
i don't feel
nor claim it
a different kind of power
this is part of whole
learning protocol
dreamed in deep breathing out hurt
understanding moon
i am sacrifice
the choice not to split in two
is one of power
last night i saw it
so clearly in tune focus
breathe into knowing
the pain lays you up
time for quiet reflection
listen now careful
for wars were won
with visions given by moon
to women bleeding
it's why they fear it
why they vanish us away
this blood wins wars

ka paɫkinińtik
or
there are things our women have taught me:
1. give generously without worrying where more will come from;
2. laugh deep and hard with each other more than you cry;
3. learn everything you can and teach it freely;
4. know where you are going and go all the way-get the doctoral degree, get on council, hell, don't stop there, you can be nasukin-you can lead your nation;
5. speak softly walk gently rock your babies to sleep;
6. raise your voice in song or anger-never be silent in the face of injustice;
7. feed everyone, including yourself;
8. light the fires, call in the drums, join hands-you never know when you'll need a friend-honour your relations;
9. share the good stories alongside the tough ones-share whatever story feels right, from the you light up my lifes to the ain't it awfuls, and especially the sexy ones-on that note
10. fall in love and celebrate every orgasm;
11. hold your loved ones close and breath in the scent of them;
12. grieve loss as deeply as you love, without shame or fear;
13. carry the hearts of your sisters your grandmothers your daughters born or yet to come your aunties and nieces and cousins-carry them in your heart;
14. keep going. This is not the end.

there's this thing happens
the not good enough kicks in
nothing you can do
nothing i can do
even if we see the lie
it drowns out the rest
we are caribou
our legs swept out from under
Elders weep for us
i weep now for us
told we're never good enough
even before birth
it keeps us from love
blood memory gushes out
pouring through fingers
your hands still too small
even clasped tight in my own
it's only triage
a makeshift stopgap
it'll only hold so long
the rivers of tears and blood

trying to stay offline
news i can't look away from
and my heart just hurts
so here's a poem
to tell you i love you and
fuck white supremacy.

reconciliation
would mean indigenous youth
growing up alive
will you reconcile?
abolish rcmp.
give us safety

i'm still from the west
and so i forgot that he
the pm with the hair
is in this city
where i am reading about
his sweeping statements
he grew up here too
in the land of parliament
only visited
the west coast so he
could surf sail and shirtless smile
i realized too
we both carry a
thunderbird or two inked deep
into our skin by
needles and i think
about what that sacrifice
means to me as my
fresh ink still itches
i cried when the first one was
finished knowing i
carry this fight for
clean water for our mother
with me til i die
i've watched him cry
big salty tears on tv
watched him hug his wife
his children are here
in this city where i slept
where i will stand with
my nation where i
will pray for better outcomes
i will pray for him

you listening, pm?
we see all the photo ops
let's see the action

a poem for notley
and the newly wine-born activist
but wine and oil are
connected in ways maybe
you can't understand
spirits that only
learn how to take
extraction
things we learn to need
industry boycotts
tools of capitalism
tools of oppression
why save the water?
to make sure the grapes are fed?
so you can stay drunk?
how did this spirit
become so deeply strengthened?
holy communion
every day self care
it's five o'clock somewhere and
hell you deserve it

one time a story
about wine and rebellion
made sense clearly
my dearest great aunt
oh how i miss her right now
sitting with old folks
in the chapel that
is just around the corner
from where i sit now
snuck in during school
(yes, the residential school)
drunk on communion
teenage rebellion
funny because i only
knew grandma sober

this isn't judgement
ancestors know i can't judge
wine
a drink of choice
a glass of red wine
the first drink that last time
i fell off the wagon

but you know something?
maybe this poem wants to
dispel a hard myth

did you know that those
same NDNs who fight pipelines
stay sober now too?
did you know we have
more sobriety in our
great nations
than you?
so think harder now
about dismantling greed
what will you give up?
what's it really worth?
this ground we walk on together
the water we drink
what would it mean to
straighten out these roads we walk?
to invest deeply
economies of care
hard critical decisions
a dismantling
i don't have answers
but thank you for reading for
thinking and perhaps
thank you the most
for supporting my new road
wine-free and dreaming
dreaming of oil-free
holding fast to this fight that's
deeply connected

how to support me today *after Orlando*

1.
do not bring up wounded knee, for that is my trauma, too. do not reach into my gunshot wound unless it is to stop the bleeding and hold the pieces of me together.

2.
do not perpetuate the hatred spat from the killer's gun with your responses. there is no space here for your racism. there is no space here for your politics. there is no space here for your words unless they can reach into this gunshot wound to stop the bleeding and hold the pieces of me together.

3.
if you are gay, lesbian, bisexual, two-spirit, trans, latinx, or anyone else who knows this violence the way we do, please take care of yourself. if you have words to share, spread them around this world and into our wounds. if you cannot speak, let your silence resonate into us. let us hold each other together our blood mixing in rainbows of love and solidarity in candlelight unburdened by fda bans on our freedom to relate to one another. let us reach into these gunshot wounds to stop the bleeding and hold the pieces of each other together.

4.
if you are white or straight or anyone to which this violence is unfamiliar, stop.
take a breath.
take another.
breathe our words into yourself.
if you must share, then share our stories. repeat our names. listen to our heartbeats and make space for us to mourn, grieve, and be with one another.
do not speak.
do not speak.
do not speak.
do not speak unless you are absolutely certain that your words can reach into our gunshot wounds and stop the bleeding. Do not act unless you know that your action will hold the pieces of us together.

5.
this one's for the grandmothers. grandfathers. aunties and uncles. for all our older relations who remain neither man nor woman but some fierce being in between. this one's for the stonewallers. for the bulldykes. for the drag queens and the elders. for all the ones who came before us. for those whose words and lives made this world feel safer, if only

for a second. for those rainbow warriors (no, not you), who raised their fists and flags and lit our way out of closets and into communities. we remember.

remember to hope. remember to dance. remember to open our bodies to the possibilities of another being, the same being, only different. wet, hard, hot, heavy, soft, juicy, thick, layered, beautiful in it's newness, incredible in it's familiarity, raw, powerful, and awesomely sexy. remember that we can reach in. we can stop the bleeding. we will hold the pieces of you together. #morelove. always.

deadliest mass shooting
the words have lost their meaning
neon in vegas
too much to notice
and yet here we are again
mourning and grieving
at shots fired in crowds
another 50 victims
countless more injured
and i think of land
of that mass of electric
in the dry desert
and i think of songs
growing up singing country
my boots and my hat
think of my first shows
terri clark and paul brandt in
my hometown arena
think of all my friends
and family who've gone there
"from vegas with love"
i will light the smudge
send prayers for all those grieving
think of Orlando
and ask folks to see
how guns made to do this will
continue their jobs

you wrote a poem
leading me to google it
where i came upon
those words he uttered
echoes of bush and iraq
"mission accomplished"
syrian children
in my heart today
with those
indigenous kids
and i dream power
dream of calling on spirits
that can help us now
dream of mountains
and the death of the monster
its body
my home
when i build my house
it will be a refuge
and
you can always come
we can cry there
too
ruminating on the state
of our sorry world
and then we'll get up
hug each other
hug the kids
smudge
and share a meal

#recovery

on depression and addiction and
"not good enough"

searching the dark room
living in the translucent
red white of skin cells
pray that this is what
recovery feels like what
renewal feels like

offer what i can
but emotional labour
takes its toll
rest now

censoring my art
is the strongest sign that the
decision i am
making or about
to is not a great idea
it starts with haiku
but could end quickly
with long gone goals returning
swallowed burning down

deep chest heart heavy
both familiar and new
hopes antithesis

and still there are days
when the poems about you
seem closer to truth
than whatever breath
of conviction you last took
whispering you've changed

depression update:
when i served tables we'd say
hey, i'm in the weeds
write me on the board
i'm eighty-sixing myself
we're all out of me

it's time now young one

they whisper urgently
sweating and shaky
eyes unable to focus

the tears come easy then stop
just as quick

i'm okay

       a lie screamed so loud

that's bullshit it's all bullshit

       the mirror begs shattering
       body begs for more
       poison beatings intrusions
       anything to fix

you are not broken young one

this time it goes unheard
they will keep repeating
the stars in clear december

you are not broken.

the moon exhales the sun

you are not broken.

a song sung low in prayer

you are not broken.

they will keep repeating
it's time now.
listen.

sometimes it's easy
gratitude and memory
mix instead of drinks
not yet always though
some days the feel of red wine
too familiar
maybe i dreamt it
and carry anxiety
into the day
maybe it's simple
i forgot to eat again
and food will fix it
either way it calls
but i am not answering
not today, okay?
so i miss the show
there will be others i don't
other parties too
solstice is a time
to say goodbye to the dark
dark that saved my life
dark almost killed me
time to greet again the light
to wake up clear here
your words mean so much
"take care of yrself, please" [heart]
thank you friend
i am
hold me and we'll sleep
our way through the darkest night
wake up beside me
as the sun rises
ill watch you prepare for day
made it through again

worst day of the year
"blue monday" they've named it
carried by sunday
take heart
take comfort
for even feeling like shit
you are not alone
just get through
my loves
in bed coughing
or weeping
holding yourself tight
at work tomorrow
or not moving from the couch
whatever it takes
please just get through it
we need you here on tuesday
we need you here
now

                                    i do not blame you.
                            just one more too many's all
                                      that separates us
                                   wish i could kill it—
                     this fucking beast that took you
                                     wish i could hurt it
                                      like it's hurting us
                                    all i can do is fight it
                                       i'll keep on fighting

you can't save them all
heavyweighted heart hurting
hope they save themselves
hope they keep fighting
hope they know how much you care
hope they see you
know
you're fighting too

and really that's it
i didn't control my life
that thing had me then
and now even though
some days feel like it's right there
waiting whispering
calling me up ring
ring
but i'm home now and just not
picking up
hang up
just hang the fuck up
because this unanswered life
is too beautiful
don't leave a message
i smashed the old machine with
a hammer threw the
pager in the air
and hit it with a dead shot
my technology
has moved on from you
this emotion reminds me
i block your number

i will let you down
a handpainted warning hung
above my bed
balanced by pastel
the blanket-star guides me home
more truth than caution
i will let you down
reflected in the mirror
where another sign
you are enough
hangs
how can both be true? you ask
if you get lucky
maybe you'll find out
you'll get to stay long enough
to see me clearly
all the haiku and
every selfie and the truth
i will let you down
you are enough

you are enough

a handwritten note on my mirror
it's been there two years
as i'm packing i think of throwing it away
it doesn't seem to have done its job

you are enough you are enough you are enough you are

if i say it ten times really fast
if i sing it to the tune of a ceremony song
if i close my eyes and use my semaa
if i envision my own hands wrapped tightly
if i envision the song as a bandage
if i can just will the bleeding to stop
if i keep trying just keep trying just keep going
if i let the tears fall
if i listen to my own all too familiar wailing
if i go for a walk
if i just breathe in and out and in and out and
if i sit with the tightness in my chest enough times
if i go to therapy like a good ptsd patient
if i envision a stop sign or a cover for the cage that my critic bird lives in
or if i take my vitamins or if i stop drinking coffee or if i open the blinds
or if i recycle or if i stop using plastic all together or if i win another
award or if i get my phd

then will it become true?

"we have everything we need"
when you said it that first time
it took everything to try and believe
but when i woke up today
angry that they tried to make me forget it
i think i understand

i am everything i need

                              and when they wake up
                        in the mornings now they smile
                              they can see themselves
                                    look in the mirror
                        i just can't seem to quit you
                              why would i want to?

keep collecting rings
will my skin to feel safer
wrapped tight in armour

                                    i thought i was safe
                              spun myself in blankets of
                              spiderwebs torn open

and i can't keep up
but just know dear that i'm
deeply grateful
for you

someday i'll look back on this
and tell a young one
there was a time i had to learn how to breathe.

and i'll teach them about how the
earth
water
inhale
exhale
stars line up

there is never enough

and i'll tell them
in many ways this is all that i know
you need to cultivate an army

you need the ones who see you
when enough is enough

the ones who lay tobacco
in the place that shares your name
the ones that text you through it
hours out of their day
the ones who hug you so tight
who show you their pain
the ones who pour a glass of water
open the door to you crying on the porch
the ones who give you a key
and let you do your thing
the ones who see you
will
remind you
who you are

remember

and i'll make it a home
cross often these wooden floors
open and draw blinds
follow the patterns
of day turned to night turned to
worn floorboard paths
and
you'll never come here
you are the uninvited
once made my body
your home but then i
took it back from your false grip
i woke up
saw you
they taught me of you
and now you'll never come here
don't bother trying
the back gate's locked
i'll stop you at the door
my body
my home
now

                              wallowing in lone
                    cut all your t-shirts to fit
                    what you're becoming
                          realize you'll fly
          back to the mountains that housed
                    you when you were young
                          only a quick trip
                    safety will be here waiting
                          your bathroom mirror
                    we laugh at rainbows
          and yet the queerness is home
                    something familiar
                    we find each other
          and we hold on for dear life
                          a quick trip
                              this time
                    i'll be back soon

sage and cigarettes
i met myself there
on the day you said i smelled
of sage and cigarettes
learned how to see me
in the dark creases made by
so many years walked
in these cowboy boots
the dust from every home
ground down
made better
saw myself here, too
in the feathers on my desk
smudge pan filled with use
felt the comfort of
deep purple high thread count sheets
a desk that says love
saw myself just now
in the grey cat curled up at
the foot of my bed

                                    and then it hits you
                              wave after wave of anguish
                                 screaming at nothing
                                  the cat looks at you
                                   you are alone now
                                            safe
                               safe safe safe safe safe
                                  still doesn't feel safe
                             it was the first time you spoke
                                           today
                                 they were irritated
                                 as always always
                         your heart bleeding on their grass
                                just helping a friend
                            when later you were asked
                            where do you feel reaction?
                               you surprised yourself
                                         nowhere
                                    i feel nothing
                             until just now at the sink
                             their voice back full force
                               and your body tenses
                          you scream your rage at nothing
                                  the cat looks at you

poem after reading an article on high functioning c-ptsd
after kesha's "praying"

a rare diagnosis sure
the pain in my shoulders tells me it's back though

                                        it never left.

it's like i become
some raw thing
skin grated down
(want to peel my skin off)
brain crackling
(want to cut my brain out)

                                        exhausting.

have you ever felt this way?
always hoping last time

                                        the very last time.

let's sit down to write
play that song on repeat

                                        for hours now

beg for new music
and still only play this song
over and over
something in her voice
reminding me of former selves

                                        wait

am i triggering self now?
re-traumatizing?
is it somehow all my fault?
(want it to be my fault)

Stop!   Turn if off!

71

but it's not the song

not my fault

not so easily

changed
fixed

healed   linear

and i've taken to constantly
brushing my shoulders off

stamping my feet

anything to protect

lay cedar at the edge of the yard

how do i protect
the edges of me?
the edge of the world

too sharp.

some days being here
means leaving dance class early
to cry in the car
means sitting with moon
listening to reminders
from new connections
felt deep in our spirits
some days being here present
is the hardest thing
deciding to stay
knowing reasons why i drank
things worth running from
i take a deep breath
and face them clear this time round
strong, sure, but in pain
some days being here
means refusing to contain it
not letting lift locks dam these waters or syllables count out my words
or fear of my upstairs neighbours thoughts quiet my heartsong as I learn
how to heal it as I learn how to sit with it as I learn how to present
myself to her, our grandmother, I ask her to see all of me the way we
get to see her change every cycle the way her light grows and darkens
as the clouds pass over her the way the ancestors dance with her and
carry her up there someday I think maybe I'll get to visit with her all
the way up there and she'll tell me she remembers that night when the
stray cat scared me as I sat in my little back yard and asked her to help
me continue to show myself to shed the layers of grief for the futures
that never came and be present in the one that is here happening now in
the body that I present to her that is not a mistake but has had too many
limits set upon it I ask her to help me break free from containment and
I think of the way she controls the waves and in some ways I understand
just what I need to do and some days I can see that being here is the
most incredible miracle and it is enough. It is so much enough. simply
being here.
migwech nokomis
husukiɬqukni ka titinaɬa

a rough couple days
sobbing i can't breathe i can't
in the studio
try to keep going
you want this you can do this
lift one more weight now
just stop crying just
stop
you've done this seven weeks
you can keep going
write the department
"come out" with the name change and
tell them your pronouns
deep fear runs through you
you, the god damn example
always the leader
sometimes all you want
is to be mediocre
a stranger somewhere
serving up coffee
in a small roadside diner
at the edge of town
sometimes you want to
disappear to the southwest
it's warm and dry there
but you can't you know
not yet anyways 'cause you
promised miss magoo
no more long car trips
and you have to keep writing
keep going
keep on

somehow you forgot
december is the hardest
they beckon you loud
over and over
just one drink
maybe you could
just one
just a little holiday
the red wine whiskey
whispers
we know you better than
anyone maybe
we'll hold you close dear
just one
maybe
and then
and then
they'll throw you to the wolves
and then and then and then
play the tape out they taught you
it never ends well
just one day one hour
just every fucking second
you could be convinced
it's still a fucking war
you still miss some version of you
distorted and ugly
you miss them still though
you miss your bar friends and your
days spent not caring
you miss you miss you
what happens if maybe you
don't make it this time?

cycle through seasons
hibernate
look back on it
hold close and stay home
you have all you need
say it over again now
repetition helps
it's only you here
you who got you this damn far
you who knows it now
nothing to do with
all the hurt disappointment
nothing to do with
them or the bright lights
nothing to do with the cold
this is just for you
the truth in this home
in the place you've created
here in this body

the change of a year
last one i opened love notes
you sent me here with
they helped get me through
before i learned who you were
before it went bad
now i can see it
that i needed your teaching
needed your love notes
sometimes we fall hard
too fast too fun feels too good
hit the ground harder
still angry sometimes
but it's rare now and fleeting
mostly forgotten
yet here i am back
these mountains holding me home
a full moon just passed
and i didn't need
your love notes this time around
i am enough
now

loneliness seeps in
remind yourself of creatures
solitary lives
remember lessons
sometimes the turtle gets smashed
sometimes
it lays eggs
be like wolverine
nobody sees you these days
unless you show them
there's a party there
in some unfamiliar
downtown toronto club
you want to go but
you told a story today
you watched an old show
one that reminds you
of 2008
of
pills
and lines
and card games
and so many tears
and promises promises
the only one kept
was the one you made
to your unborn nephew then
"i promise i'll stay."
and you did
you know
you stayed to meet him
and now
he just turned seven
and here you are
eating chocolate cake instead
of going out
this time
here you are
alive
and you can live with it now
the loneliness
now

and all night dreams of
drinking
of assholes in bars
questioning my name
you introduced me
with the wrong name
while you drank
and i decided
enough was enough
i couldn't last anymore
sat down at a bar
and old friends were there
and there was too much explaining
woke up exhausted
when you quit something
no
when you quit coping
no
when you quit using
that thing you always used to
cope
with everything
there's a fear that stays
lingering
one that says
you'll never be okay
there's a fear too though
that maybe
you will be
and that
might be the hardest

it was a whole life
despite the newly minted
birth certificate
it was a whole life
as i get deep in albums
posted years ago
i see 'her' and cry
so many tears for that 'girl'
never comfortable
remove tag
delete
think of the conversation
in orillia
do we take it down?
the monuments of
colonialism?
do i deny 'her'?
erase the evidence of
'her' unhappy life
people like to ask
will i cut parts of 'her' off?
oh but how i did
always cutting off
suffocating my spirit
drowning out my fire
i look at 'her' now
and cry for the hidden me
under so much pain
uncomfortable clothes
lipstick and hangovers and
that man i was with
thank you kulilu
for the teachings you bring us
caterpillar
too
still turning to mush
still needing to build cocoon
to find a safe nest
still always changing
still transitioning
just as we all are
always

and dysphoria
changes faces always
too
today's memory
bringing a smile
laugh
"holy she was a babe, hey?"
some days it's okay
still "she" isn't me
but some days it's maybe "we"
maybe it's they / them
because that's fluid
not some here to there journey
never linear
her and i
we are
layers of time and spirit
sage and cigarettes
birth certificates
really only register
colonially
i wish i could scream
it's not even about gender
i just want to scream
we are not the same
intersectionality
feels like
i can't breathe
and yet i see her
and today
smiled at memory
we did have some fun
everything she did
all that happened to her
all that happened to
me

after days of "she"
it takes practice to see
me
camera timers
so many selfies
searching for the truth of it
in my eyes
arms
hands
and don't forget him
that guy on the street today
who yelled out "hey, bro"
you think it's so hard
and yet i think if i could
make you feel that good
with the change of just
one word
i'd do anything
i just know i would

and i lied to you
never told the whole truth
shared traumas quiet
so that maybe now
when i can't get outta bed
nothing to tell you
all i see is dark
this system we're locked into
power over us
when i'm just tired
when i don't have hope to
hold onto
to share
when i looked today
for things like yellow
or fire
and still couldn't see
maybe now you can
remember what i told you
tried to warn you
that painting hanging
above my bed i will
always let you down
so many reasons
why i've made it here
this far
and all of them
start with
alone

seventeen months
"i'm proud of you."
my new therapist always
knows what to say
quieting the doubt
that sometimes still lingers dark
in corners of me
am i man enough
if you choose not to see me
am i good enough
this week marks thirty
years
in this body
on earth
this week marks five months
of new medicine
changing it ever slowly
deepening my voice
growing my desire
for a simple life
quiet
and this week
it marks
seventeen whole months
since i kicked that spirit out
sobriety
now
a birthday party
i would have avoided then
scoffed at not drinking
ashamed for so long
working so hard to die young
and yet
here i am
never thought i'd be
twenty three even
never
imagined
thirty

remember that time
instead of drinking
you called
on your army
and
then climbed a mountain
remember what it felt like
all alone up there?

#ceremony

on coming home

i had forgotten
the kiss of the prairie moon
so near horizon
lightning spirits dance
along the path south
always
the numa follows
tonight i am safe
tomorrow
a returning
another heart home

i tell her my dreams
of course we are connected
me
you
family

this must be the place
black sky softest pelt of snow
leads the clearest moon

dining room table
soft pine with the markings of
a twelve-year-old me
carved with a pencil
through the paper into wood
traced with dad's fingers
the spirit of home
river rocks make the chimney
a place i do love
moved so far away
grateful to be reminded
by your love for trees
tonight

tap snow off cedar
prepare in quiet prayer
do what keeps you warm

ceremony days
darkening skin strengthening
all our relations

somedays the knowledge
asks me not to share it
even at the fire
even in tipis
(maybe especially there)
everything we do
everything we do
is political he said
i understand now
it's not that we try
we just in essence become
space of extraction
be careful young ones
they don't just seek the water
oil land trees they name
resources (relations)
they will try to take your heart
they will mine your body
bleed you dry and ask
for more more more they want more
remember to pray
remember that we
carry saying no in our
dna and that
we are allowed
no
we are responsible for
protecting ourselves
protecting knowledge
protecting ways of knowing
protecting future

we've lost it somehow
the art of visiting
he said it quietly
my heart made a vow
"take it up again" they spoke
"now when it feels tough"
as they do they did
not warn me to be careful
lessons told before
go unsaid to teach
so when i forgot was taught
again and again
exhausted quiet
"remember how to visit"
i heard aki+wi
there are those who take
but they only win if we
in response stop giving
so gather your gifts
and seek out those to practice
some will prove too much
but you'll find magic
they'll invite you in to their homes
offer their beauty
wrapped in care for you
gently it fills you up and
you offer it back

after gitiga migizi

electric powwow
but you didn't see me there
quiet night instead
in ceremony
listening for what to do
ancestors' whispers
ka ha¢a is sick
fever dreams tell him of us
youth with work to do
see you at jump dance
ka ¢u (i don't know yet how
to say you're younger)

never read silko
learn ceremony right here
too many matches
if you hold it down
it's more likely it will catch
need to know basis
keep our voices low
some days we do different
always together
i know you're upset
siblings generous with time
we each have a role

what's so sacred about four?

we are in a native lit class
my piikani sister and i
connected
internally rolling our eyes

"i don't know"
when the prof looks to me
ka ¢u with a better answer
still uncomfortable

if you asked me today
i would tell you
four years ago
i went into my first sweat

it must have been a full moon
snow in vancouver
my suyapi friend
a close one

invited me in
she works hard to bring
connection to those
who need it most

last night
i'd tell you
we came out of a sweat
full moon snow on the ground

i don't count anymore
but it was the first
for my sisters
who we invited in

five months
wake up in the bed i came here for a year ago
hear you laugh downstairs and smile
at the familiar way the sun comes through this window
at the tree i say good morning to
cupcakes and root beer floats
my anxiety now from a missing kid on tv
i only watch the scary shows here
surrounded by my family
there are new understandings
there are hotter sweats
there are siblings i get to know better
and of course there's the anxious dog
there's that grocery store with two sections of everything
my deep fear of ticks my deep love
of the visiting scholars we call family
there's the hippy market and there's the gorges
learning family the way i learn this place
driving around telling our stories
sometimes getting lost along the way
the spirits calling us home

five stages they say
and in the morning you wake
rage shaking your hands
want to get on stage
scream like a white band front man
who knows they'll listen
block a few people
unfollow more
(politics)
dream of driving off
back to mountains
way out west where you came from
dreaming of sweat rocks
burdens too heavy
for you to carry for them
cry for the young ones
and the old ones too
and then breathe into the rage
remember back then
when you used to scoff
at the words "idle"
"sleeping"
you carried respect
and now you see it
we are weak and pitiful
they've let you down
scared you'll do it too
pray hard into the rage now
that you are enough

ceremony time
opens hearts and spirit up
that real world layer
and sometimes they play
sometimes they might whisper things
learn to listen
ceremony time
once you told me
babies
come on those cycles
post-dance gestation
'cause of that pow wow trail glow
firelight
smell of smoke
we are all filled up
each beautiful spirit seen
in ceremony time

the stars they told me
keep doing what you're doing
boundary-making
shedding old skin cells
let go of what holds you down
and look out for love
that kind of bright spark
bursting upwards
new flame
as
the fire takes a breath
that full moon told me
to ask for healing cleaning
cedar bath at sunrise
getting to know self
in the quiet moments here
look out to the yard
this place you've built
home
and know you'll go west soon too
know who you are
here
the mountains told me
carry knowing in your body
dream this knowing home

feel tips of your wings
across the small of my back
push smoke into me
the fire takes a breath
there's that same line repeating
as i think of her
her song
a few bars
stuck in my head now for weeks
smile plays on my lips
the fire takes a breath
learning balance this weekend
make peace between them
fire and water
unless you are like me
"it's different" auntie told us
radical balance
we move in spaces between
and the medicine
the medicine helps
my fire—
then
it was drowning
now i feel it breathe

and you'll keep the fire
and we'll tell stories sing songs
wake to greet the sun

#forandafter

to those who've gone before
and some of you still here,
i love you

for cw

today we gather
bring our power together
send it out to the
water our mother
the plants land animals
all our relations
today we gather
out of fear anger hurt hope
but most of all love
it's the fiercest love
love we will lay our bodies
down for will die for
love for those to come
a love we want you to know
love for those who came
like odenabe
the river we gather with
like the old warped tree
like the grandmothers
and grandfather rocks circling
like the centre fire
we are here alive
like those protectors southwest
we are important
we have work to do
we are necessary by
way of our creation

after ls
reach into the universe
feel the stars spark static at your touch
we are all connected

as the fresh-faced earth
turns to meet light once more
another Creation story beginning

maybe you crossed my path once
on a bus in a city i inhabited
maybe i sang to you from a christmas-lit stage

you wore my old uniform
we danced at a wedding for a friend
neither of us talk to anymore

there's a tree they say
is the oldest one here
but it can't be the oldest one anywhere

i hear your thoughts sometimes
alongside my own
the nascent space of my beliefs

colonized by your constant lacking
my all-encompassing wonder
silenced

with the sharp snap of your interruption
she sings to that oldest tree
they've been here millennia

and she sings the songs of this place
she sees me knows i am from here too
my umbilical cord incinerated in some garbage dump

how could a foster mother keep them all?
what would she do with them?
and so i am in the air here

and so the oldest tree breathes me
breathes in her song
and the stars listen as we comfort each other

they feast as we feast
drink the water of galaxies
odenabe

the blood water of your heart
a dewdrop
on the leaf of

the oldest tree in the world

woke today to see
a good morning message from
you
who helped me cry
yesterday when i
still didn't know how to
be here
in this world
woke today to see
photos of your new tattoo
lines inked into skin
represent family
thread looped into you tying
you back
blood and ink
ancestral memory
i woke today and thought of
the message you sent
the other day that
talked of that hungry spirit
what it will do
told me of its smile
and i realized you wrote
so much in warning
i read every one
every story you
gave us
taught us how to fight
i woke this morning
tired and sore
but still here
the moon
new again

for CrisQo

we were just young kids
and you never got older
it's strange to think of
last time i was home
i left a couple smokes by
your bench at the park
i hope some punk ass
skater kid found them and read
your name i hope he
smiled and lit one up
and heard pink floyd on the air
before dropping in

after SC

i lay in the crook
body formed in the mattress
breathe medicine smoke
stare through the orange
white green mandala hanging
memories of you
wonder if the land
will hold onto me like this
drink in my decay
when i become dust
glitter visiting with stars
call me with fingers
tousled through your hair
pushed deep into the earth's soil
becoming our mother

after dm

your fingerprints have
oxidized themselves
onto copper piping

the map of your skin
you use to ochre the walls
to print names in blood

there's something sacred
something sacrificial
here in this room of

unbroken eye lines
there are four photos
four clear offerings

imagine your hands
shaping these medicine gifts
while i watch the moon

the same way you would
hold semaa in your hands
offer it to land

for cc
after ee

i carry your heart
(i carry it in my heart)
ee etched into
our arms (the left ones)
scrawled down the veins to our hands
where i hold semaa
(tobacco) when i
pray for your heart (i carry)
back home we just lost
a bright young paɬki
(woman) and i cry and smudge
and think of you too
you who cries like me
medicine tears softening
this hard angry world

for cj

last night i took time
to breathe deep into the song
i took every chance
i drove the band home
this morning i remember
you'd be twenty-eight
holding memory
is an honour and a gift
as you still teach me
to smile every day
to pet every dog i see
to practice my skills
to share my stories
to invite my friends to play
and eat together
you taught me about
love family and of course
loss
that loss taught me
to appreciate and live
it to the fullest
happiest birthday
my dear friend
thank you
for every gift

after tw

the loons are calling
as we keep each other warm
about to take flight
lips brush powder soft
snow light touch of your wings
fluttering half-beat
learning loyalty
curling up into the moon
into me breathe close
river time lapses
a flash an eternity
this calm lifting off

for michelle

and things fell apart
woke up 4am shiver
furnace light gone out
your name not here yet
whispering to me today
my cousin
my dear one
you were what age then
just twenty-two
i think you were
twenty two years young
and me at fourteen
how could i have known it then
last time i saw you
things they fall apart
some people
they don't wake up
only twenty-two
and there i am now
hear grandmas wailing
your grave
she's gone since then
too
and i just miss you
i just
wish there was more
wish i could go back
body remembers
each part of me wanting now
to follow you there
yesterday so hard
i wondered why
still forgot
until i saw the date
i wrote you that song
sang about feeling you here
please stay
please stay
please

for sk (my good friend)

and then everything
slows down and you are back in
your own home
own bed
and your cat is here
sleeping in her orange chair
like maybe nothing
ever happened
though
you know better than that
dear
yes
you know better
you were there for days
for the orange pop requests
for all those last smiles
you were there even
then
in the final moments
and there
days after
and your life has changed
in knowing more deeply now
what it means to live
anishinaabe
mno bimaadiziwin
what it means to die
anishinaabe
what it means to be here now
to be here for this
to sit keeping watch
to honour relations
right to the body's
end.

a love poem to your great great grandmother

ka titinała
the one that started it all
though i have a feeling you'd say
there was another before you
but this poem is for you
whose prayers were so strong
done in just the right way
hidden away in a drawer
for so many years waiting
for the right moment
the right granddaughter
the right ceremony
right is the wrong word for this
maybe i believe in
ordination
if only when i think of you
when i think of him
here with us
breathing
typing out his own love poems
honouring
this family that saved his life
husukiłqukni
thank you
for bringing all that you have
ick sukapi
thank you
for saving my life
nya:wen
thank you
for sharing your family
your teachings
your presence
gineehayan
thank you
for praying us here

for carol warrior

for ka manał̓a
our mother
for you
sun dancer
thank you feels too small
gineeheyaan much closer
our hearts opened up
a new presence found
taught us how to love
taught us how to fight
beauty surrounds us
that fierce love of creation
each tiny moment
and most important
our place within it all
"you have a place here"
"you are enough."